ROCK 'N' ROLL WOMEN

Portraits of a Generation

ROCK 'N' ROLL WOMEN

Portraits of a Generation

NEW POEMS BY
Jonah Raskin

McCaa Books • Santa Rosa

Copyright © 2012 by Jonah Raskin
All rights reserved

Without limiting the rights under copyright reserved above, no part of this publication may be reproduced, distributed, or transmitted in any form or by any means, or stored in a database or retrieval system, without the prior written permission of both the copyright owner and the publisher of this book except in the case of brief quotations embodied in critical articles or reviews.

ISBN 978-0-9838892-3-6

First published in 2012 by McCaa Books,
an imprint of McCaa Publications.

Cover Design: James Retherford/Hot Digital Dog Design

Cover Photographs: Vladimir Nikulin

Printed in the United States of America
Set in Minion Pro

McCaa Books
1535 Farmers Lane #211
Santa Rosa, CA 95405-7535
www.mccaabooks.com

Dedicated to the *ones* I love

CONTENTS

Introduction	9
Marie & Creedence	11
Sally & Ricky Nelson	12
Sue & Elvis	13
Liz & The Everly Brothers	14
Ellen & The Beatles	15
Angelica & Janis Joplin	16
Joan & Joe Cocker	17
Judy & The Doors	18
Paula & Sly Stone	19
Anita & Carole King	20
Karen & Ry Cooder	21
Penny & The Joy of Cooking	22
Hannah & Jimmy Cliff	23
Tamara & Otis Redding	24

Contents

Rita & Tina Turner	25
Louisa & Bob Dylan	26
Mr. Tommy & Mick Jagger	27
Alicia & Pat Benatar	28
Sadie & Beach Boys/Sex Pistols	29
Linda & The Grateful Dead	30
Margaret & Pink Floyd	31
Ashley & Roseanne Cash	32
Monica & Beyoncé	33
Bernadette & All the Rock 'n' Rollers	34
All Together Now	35
Jonah Raskin's Short List of Selected Rock 'n' Roll CDs	37
Acknowledgments	39

INTRODUCTION

Rock 'n' Roll Is Here to Play

ROCK 'N' ROLL BROKE INTO MY LIFE when a teenage girl older than I blasted Bo Diddley on her record player. She was a dishwasher with curly hair. I heard the music come out of her bedroom window and could not get it out of my head. Later, at school at lunch hour in the gym when guys danced with girls, I heard Carl Perkins and I haven't been the same person since. I had grown up on folk music and on rhythm and blues—I played Leadbelly records everyday for a year— and rock 'n' roll sounded in my ears as though it had come out of black bars, the black ghetto, and the juke joints of the South.

Soon after the British Invasion of the 1960s, when rock 'n' roll bands such as the Beatles and the Stones, came to the States, I went to England and lived with an American who played the guitar and sang the blues in British pubs. When I came back home and started teaching literature, I attended rock concerts on campus with tens of thousands of students and heard The Beach Boys, the Jefferson Airplane, and other bands. Mostly, I listened to rock 'n' roll with others, rarely by myself, and often in the company of women, many of whom show up in these poems and to whom I mean to remember and

Introduction

to pay homage. Moreover, I wrote these poems explicitly for the purpose of performing them in public and so I have paid particular attention to the sounds of the words on the page. Hopefully you'll hear music in the background even when you read this work quietly at home.

About thirty women show up in *Rock 'n' Roll Women* plus one man. I didn't want to leave men out completely; some might say that the one man I have included isn't a very good example of American manhood. To that I would say, I am not trying to provide good examples of anything. Rather, I aim to capture a specific person, place, and time from the 1950s to the present day when I'm still likely to listen to rock 'n' roll on CD or on radio stations such as KWMR that broadcasts from Point Reyes Station in Marin and that must know that I'm listening and that there are others out here beside me who want to hear rock 'n' roll, too.

Jonah Raskin
February 2012

Jonah Raskin

MARIE & CREEDENCE

Would you still boogie,
cry aloud with Creedence?
Hell you would, Marie!
So, dig out the faded scrapbooks,
break out Grace Slick & Madonna,
Bobby Darin & Nirvana,
dial up Maybelline & Peggy Sue,
linger over Polaroids.
Strange now how flawless you looked
in bobby sox & berets,
Rock 'n' Roll woman.

Rock 'n' Roll Women

SALLY & RICKY NELSON

Wham, bam, slam
back of the movie house,
in the alley, Sally,
after makin' out
with James Dean
on the screen,
cherry cokes, greasy burgers,
your ruby lips,
his hot car,
Ricky Nelson on the radio,
Rock 'n' Roll woman.

Jonah Raskin

SUE & ELVIS

Letters by mail that rend his heart,
you, Sue, at college, and so far apart.
He's listening to Elvis,
you're dating somebody else
in the frat house,
looking for a diamond ring and
he's at home alone,
dancing with you in the dark,
Rock 'n' Roll woman.

Rock 'n' Roll Women

LIZ & THE EVERLY BROTHERS

You whispered Russian, Liz, in his ear,
read aloud from Tolstoy, Turgenev
on the subway uptown, downtown,
Greenwich Village, too, and in your pad
by the banks of the Hudson.
The Everly Brothers crooning
on the wall above your bed,
taking you out of your head,
beyond the angst and
the Beat of you,
Rock 'n' Roll woman.

Jonah Raskin

ELLEN & THE BEATLES

Your guitar, an old Martin,
your hair, raven black,
you, Ellen, held his rough hands,
braved the Beatles,
raced downhill fast,
tip-toed round your mother,
swayed to his rhythm
without his blues,
wriggled, reeled on the floor,
no way you would or could ever stop,
Rock 'n' Roll woman.

Rock 'n' Roll Women

ANGELICA & JANIS JOPLIN

You, Angelica, bought tickets
to hear Janis Joplin at the Fillmore and
could hardly believe the
hurricane that hit the
stage, that blew the audience
into the back row of the balcony,
then brought them back
for a big piece of her heart and
you walked home to Avenue A
in a trance,
Rock 'n' Roll woman.

Jonah Raskin

JOAN & JOE COCKER

Broken glass,
the black of night,
the drums in the street,
the stereo in your head,
you, Joan, and your lover
stealing secret nights
in stolen bedrooms,
Joe Cocker flapping in the wind,
outside your bathroom window,
dreaming other dreams,
Rock 'n' Roll woman.

Rock 'n' Roll Women

JUDY & THE DOORS

In-between the lilac sheets,
the smell of tear gas and
patchouli,
the world you've known
crashing down
with The Doors and
the hell of Huey helicopters
on the nightly news,
fixed bayonets aimed at
your raging heart, Judy,
Rock 'n' Roll woman.

Jonah Raskin

Paula & Sly Stone

Did you smoke pot
in the beginning?
You wonder and don't remember,
though you do remember
that first acid trip
you took, Paula, along ragged shore,
your whole body
magnified immensely,
leopard-like and lusty,
stoned to Sly Stone,
Rock 'n' Roll woman.

ANITA & CAROLE KING

"Oral sex," did somebody say?
Who went down on whom, Anita?
Who clocked the hours and
sent the dead flowers?
Carole King crooning
in the pine cabin behind
the pine mountains,
naked and natural,
homemade, whole wheat bread,
balling in pretty pink pick-up truck,
Rock 'n' Roll woman.

Jonah Raskin

KAREN & RY COODER

The country wasn't big enough
or wide enough to play the music,
eight-track stereo,
on roads that wound round
lost lakes, haunted highways,
rains, floods in Minnesota,
Ry Cooder in Oklahoma,
dust bowl blues again, Karen,
turning back pages of Kerouac and
kissing along Snake River,
Rock 'n' Roll woman.

Rock 'n' Roll Women

PENNY & THE JOY OF COOKING

You gazed at glorious Golden Gate,
at bodacious brown hills of Marin
in regenerating June,
stayed tuned to KSAN and to
the strange bright light of California,
The Joy of Cooking cooking
along the barbecued shore,
you, Penny, rollicking in the sand,
frolicking with dolphins & sharks,
San Francisco Bay,
Rock 'n' Roll woman.

Jonah Raskin

H*ANNAH* & J*IMMY* C*LIFF*

The all-night rhythm parties,
snorting coke in the Mission,
Jimmy Cliff in your head,
reggae all round your bed.
Was sex as true
as you, Hannah, swore it was,
when time turned tricks,
went backwards and fast-forwards?
Or a frantic illusion that
whored you and bored you?
Rock 'n' Roll woman.

Rock 'n' Roll Women

TAMARA & OTIS REDDING

Would you be more discreet?
Please don't strew
lover's true letters on tables, chairs,
for everyone to find, not blind,
and itch, Bitch?
Otis Redding on the turntable and
you at the end of your dock,
rock 'n' roll is all you've got
to get you up when you're
this far down, Tamara,
Rock 'n' Roll woman.

Jonah Raskin

R*ITA* & T*INA* T*URNER*

He played in a garage band!
You, Rita, wanted to be a star,
took voice lessons,
groped round to be a groupie,
until he ditched you in Las Vegas,
behind the stage and
you wandered home alone,
mumbling Tina Turner lyrics,
without makeup or make believe,
begging your man "Please, take me back,"
Rock 'n' Roll woman.

Rock 'n' Roll Women

LOUISA & BOB DYLAN

Did you really download Dylan
all day every day, replay,
push the self-pity button,
sit in the dark at the Roxy,
watch *The Big Sleep* with
salty, buttery popcorn
until you, Louisa, fell asleep.
Usher woke you, roused you
sent you home in taxi and you
washed, dried sadness away,
Rock 'n' Roll woman.

Jonah Raskin

MR. TOMMY & MICK JAGGER

Where was the guy, Mr. Tommy,
through all these tunes & times?
Why, he lived in limbo, man,
drank carpenter beer at the bar,
played the last jukebox in
Nowheresville, U.S.A.
Mick Jagger's way, his way.
Met a waitress in a ponytail,
got the clap,
coulda been worse,
Rock 'n' Roll man.

Rock 'n' Roll Women

ALICIA **& P**AT **B**ENATAR

You turned back to night school,
cracked textbooks,
put on pounds,
studied chemistry,
busted caboose loose Pat Benatar,
gave biology your best shot,
hiked Saturday hills,
crammed Sunday thrills,
courses nearly sucked you dry,
but you, Alicia, scored straight A's,
Rock 'n' Roll woman.

Jonah Raskin

SADIE & BEACH BOYS/SEX PISTOLS

Bopping 'bout the bars,
solitary sister, Sadie,
sassy, spunky self,
with bank loan,
to buy big house, then
promise to be true eternally,
to rock 'n' roll guy
living in vinyl past,
Beach Boys, Sex Pistols
his/hers rock 'n' roll fantasy,
Rock 'n' Roll woman.

Rock 'n' Roll Women

LINDA & THE GRATEFUL DEAD

When did it happen, mother?
When did the day arrive?
When did you, Linda, stop looking back,
just looked ahead with
curious eye of your own kids,
hearing Grateful Dead first time,
wanting to know now what you knew
'bout Jerry then,
how he died, where, and when,
had to hear it from your ruby lips,
Rock 'n' Roll woman.

Jonah Raskin

MARGARET & PINK FLOYD

You, Margaret, cooked winter stew,
grew tarragon and didn't rue,
made tapes of Pink Floyd,
broke down dad's resistance,
reluctance to love, cut alternating
currents that drove him to extremes,
wild dreams,
acted out on crazy stage
your mother so kindly crafted,
Rock 'n' Roll woman.

Rock 'n' Roll Women

ASHLEY & ROSEANNE CASH

Your daughter, Ashley, looks like you,
sounds like you: it's uncanny.
Dances the way you once danced to
live bands, sweaty nights,
fights like you, too, behind wheel of
her own black Cadillac,
Roseanne Cash on CD,
her eyes on blue highway ahead,
you asleep in back seat,
Rock 'n' Roll woman.

Jonah Raskin

MONICA & BEYONCÉ

Listening to "Beautiful Liar"
you, you, you, Monica, fell for Beyoncé,
ached to be her lover,
inhale her big hair,
kiss her satin skin,
bring her body into your bed,
rescue her from rain and pain,
mimic her moves and her groves,
work it in and work it out with Jay-Z,
go note for note with Lady Gaga,
Rock 'n' Roll woman.

Rock 'n' Roll Women

BERNADETTE & ALL THE ROCK 'N' ROLLERS

How do you, Bernadette, not grow old?
You're not made to up and fold,
nor shrink from silence or from cold.
Rock 'n' Roll
delivered you bold from
dark days oh so cold,
bloomed you, groomed you.
Now, don silver shoes for dancin',
and, yes, a little romancin',
Hail, hail,
Rock 'n' Roll woman.

Jonah Raskin

ALL TOGETHER NOW

We've heard them play and
maybe they've played us, too,
for frantic fans and fools perhaps, but
haven't we made whole
meals of melodies,
mixed sex, drugs,
rock 'n' roll,
recipes for memory and desire,
set our bones on fire,
Rock 'n' Roll women.

Jonah Raskin's Short List of Selected Rock 'n' Roll CDs

THERE ARE TOO MANY CDs to list them all; here are some of my favorites. I am not a purist, either, and while some listeners are, I don't think rock 'n' roll is music for purists. It's wild, it's raunchy, it's loud, it's got a beat and often though not always you wanna get up and dance to it. Rock 'n' roll goes right to the body and the soul.

AC/DC, *Back in Black*

Beach Boys, *Pet Sounds*

Beatles, *Abbey Road*

Beyoncé, *Dangerously in Love*

Roseanne Cash, *Seven Year Ache*

Creedence Clearwater Revival, *Chronicle*

Jimmy Cliff, *The Harder They Come*

Joe Cocker, *Classic Cocker*

Ry Cooder, *Bop Till You Drop*

Bo Diddley, *I'm a Man*

Doors, *Best of the Doors*

Bob Dylan, *Highway 61 Revisited*

Everly Brothers, *Cadence Classics*

Selected Rock 'n' Roll CDs

Grateful Dead, *Workingman's Dead*
Janis Joplin, *Pearl*
Jefferson Airplane, *Got a Revolution!*
Joy of Cooking, *Back to Your Heart*
Carole King, *Tapestry*
Madonna, *Immaculate Collection*
Ricky Nelson, *Best of Ricky Nelson*
Nirvana, *In Utero*
Pink Floyd, *Dark Side of the Moon*
Sex Pistols, *Never Mind the Bhangra*
Elvis Presley, *The Essential Elvis Presley*
Otis Redding, *Dock of the Bay*
Sly Stone, *Sly and the Family Stone*
Rolling Stones, *Between the Buttons*
Tina Turner, *Private Dancer*
Warren Zevon, *Excitable Boy*

ACKNOWLEDGMENTS

Books take time and friends and collaborators and this book is no exception. I deeply appreciate my collaborators on and for this book including Waights Taylor Jr. the publisher, Jim Retherford, the Austin, Texas designer of the front and back cover. My hat is off to Lin Marie deVincent, the Sonoma poet, who copy edited the manuscript. I want to thank Sarah Baker, Susan Swartz, and Ed Coletti for their blurbs, Timothy Williams for accompanying me on drums when I performed these poems, and Jan Martinelli who backed me up on stand-up bass. I want to thank the local musicians, especially Stacey and Kristen of the uninhibited Penny Hens, Paul Greenley, the guitar genius, and the men who make up Mr. December. My appreciation also goes out to local poets, Elizabeth Herron, a master of public performance, Geri DiGiorno for her work on behalf of the Petaluma Poetry Walk, as well as her own poetry, and Bill Vartnaw, the most recent in a long and illustrious line of poet laureates that began with my dear, dear friend, Don Emblen, who printed at the Clamshell Press many of my poems as broadsides. Hey, strike up the band. It's time to boogie once again.

JR

ABOUT THE POET

Jonah Raskin has been writing poetry since the 1950s, when he went to high school, played football, and listened to rock 'n' roll—like the Beat Generation writers, Jack Kerouac and Allen Ginsberg whom he admired and aimed to imitate. He is the author of *American Scream*, a biography of Ginsberg's poem *Howl*, and the author, too, of six poetry chapbooks: *More Poems, Better Poems*; *Bone Love*; *Public Places, Private Spaces*; *Auras*; *Jonah Raskin's Greatest Hits*; and *Letters to a Lover*.

Raskin has also written a number of books including *The Mythology of Imperialism*; *Out of the Whale*; *The Weather Eye*; *Puerto Rico*; *Homecoming*; *My Search for B. Traven*; *For the Hell of It*; *American Scream*; *Natives, Newcomers, Exiles, Fugitives*; *The Radical Jack London*; and *Field Days*.

Raskin's latest book, *Marijuanaland*, was published in 2011. He lives in Santa Rosa, California.

www.ingramcontent.com/pod-product-compliance
Lightning Source LLC
Chambersburg PA
CBHW022347040426
42449CB00006B/766